The People's His

Chirton And Percy Main

by Pat Hope

Alice Guthrie Rippeth (aged 17) outside her home on West Percy Road in 1950.

Grace Rippeth (aged 10 or 11 years old) outside Spring Gardens School around 1945.

Previous page: Joseph Rippeth in the Royal Navy around 1919. Joseph was born on 21st September 1899 in Winlaton. He was a carpenter by trade and married Grace Foster from The Allotments in December 1925. She was working in domestic service for a family in Carlton Terrace in Whitley Bay until she married. They lived at Upper Toll Street until 1934, they moved to Peartree Crescent on the Ridges Estate.

Copyright © Pat Hope 2001

First published in 2001 by

The People's History Ltd
Suite 1
Byron House
Seaham Grange Business Park
Seaham
Co. Durham
SR7 0PY

ISBN 1 902527 75 5

Contents

Three important buildings here for the use of the public: the Meadow Well Clinic built in 1969, The Collingwood Youth Club and The Barn.

The Barn on Waterville Road in the 1980s. It was originally the Ridges Reservoir House or Ridges Waterworks. It was built around 1861 with James Hall and his wife Ann being tenants. The last tenants recorded were Walter and Mary Watson in 1973.

Introduction

This is my second book of memories of the past in photographs from local folk. My first was on the area around the Meadow Well, however, I have expanded to include the neighbouring areas of Balkwell, Chirton, West Chirton and Percy Main for this second volume.

The histories you will find through the pages are a follow up from my first book. The photographs I have received have been very intriguing and a pleasure to display.

I would like to thank all those people who have given me their deepest memories of their loved ones and their childhood days, without them this book would not exist.

The information in this book was given to me in good faith and there is no guarantee of absolute accuracy. I hope you, the reader, have as much pleasure looking through the photographs in this book as I have had in collecting and selecting them.

Pat Hope
Meadow Well, 2001

A postcard of the Albert Edward Dock sent 12th May 1919.

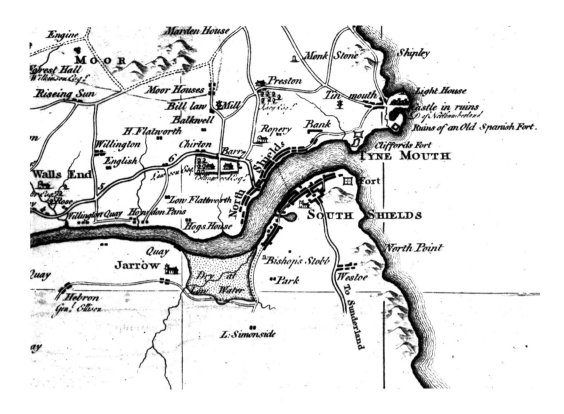

Extract of Armstrong's map of Northumberland 1769, covering the areas around North Shields. Kind permission from Newcastle City Library.

A Brief History

The area west of North Shields is where my inspiration comes from: Chirton, Percy Main, Meadow Well and Balkwell.

Each area has its own piece of history:

Chirton has been around for many years. It was a rustic village, peaceful to many who visited. It had its famous celebrities in its time – Ralph Gardner, a brewer who fought for his beliefs and for the Shields folk, to escape from the influence of Newcastle. The Duke of Argyll, Archibald Campbell, a Duke who gave William of Orange and his wife Mary the crowns of England, lived at Chirton Hall for a short time. This was a stopping place while he was on his travels from London to Argyllshire. And, not least, Lord Cuthbert Collingwood, a naval officer, who through his inheritance gained Chirton House and lands around Chirton. He never came home to live in it, only his wife and two daughters stayed.

Percy Main has changed over the last twenty years, with demolition of much of the old houses and railways. Completely covered are the scars of the old pits which were once a lifeline to many who lived there. Two hundred years or so ago, Percy Main was once called, 'a city of seven lamps' which says much about Percy Main long ago.

Meadow Well, formerly the Ridges, has had 67 years of community life and has changed in many ways from the time it was built. Amenities once essential to the early lifestyle of the estate, Ridges Reservoirs, Ridges Methodist Mission, Smiths Park and shops which filled up the main shopping area of Marina Avenue and Bridge Road South, have now disappeared.

Balkwell is an estate like Meadow Well named after the farms in their area and as like Meadow Well, had its own well. The Balkwell began in 1914, only a few short months before war broke out. Building work ceased until 1918 or 1919 when the Borough Council carried on with their original plans. St Peter's Church was built in 1930 to give their neighbours spiritual guidance.

West Chirton Estate was built in 1947, next to the Balkwell. The folk on the estate were adequately secure; schools were almost at their back doors – St Joseph's Roman Catholic School and Church in Chirton. West Chirton Industrial Estate was up and running with a wide choice of employment in the factories. Front Street Chirton and Wallsend Road had a variety of shops, an ideal place to live with no worry of travelling far for any essentials of food and clothing.

An advert for North Tyneside Co-operative Bakery Ltd on the corner of Front Street and Silkeys Lane in 1949.

Acknowledgements

Nora Thompson
Margaret (Peggy) Morgan
Beryl English
Linda Graham
Ethel Walker
Joan Bell
Alice Auchterlonie
Ann Marr
Min & Johnny Roper
Paul Crosby
Yvonne Robinson
Amanda Nathan
Norman Bishop
Una Sproston
David Hope
Joan Stevenson
Lee Bennali
Ann Watson
Maria Marsh
Linda Nathan
G.T. Park
Annette Wind
Elaine Andrews
David Beldon

Ellen Heads
Jean Bean
Paul Bine
Elizabeth Rodgerson
Julie Heads
Jean Peacock
Pat Appleton
Cathy Ellis
Jean Gilgallon
Albert & Irene Porter
Olive Jones
Jean & John Horton
Edwin Arkley
Doreen Edwards
Victoria Storey
Yvonne & Joe Howe
Margaret Lyall
Margaret Grant
Michael Marsh
Karen Fittes
Jessie Warrener
Iris Hitchcock
Yvonne Robson

A special thanks to:
Eric Hollerton and Alan Hildrew
The Local Studies, North Shields Central Library

Rev Charles Hope, St John's Church
Tony Patterson, The People's Centre
Lynne Craggs, St Peter's Church Hall
Steve Conlan, Waterville Youth Project
Canon Alec Barass, St Joseph's RC Church
Sister Michael, St Joseph's RC School
Rev David Peel, Cedarwood Trust
Margaret Nolan, Cedarwood Trust
Sheila Auld, Cedarwood Trust
Newcastle City Library

Bibliography

Evening News
Shields Daily News
Trade Directories

Published in association with North Tyneside Libraries.

CHIRTON AND

ITS PEOPLE

Chirton Cottage and Ralph Gardner Memorial at Chirton Green, *circa* 1910.
Chirton Cottage was the home of John Foster Spence from the 1860s to 1917.
He was an active campaigner for the Tyne Improvement Commission. John
Robert Hogg was elected Alderman as his successor who uprooted from 21
Linskill Terrace, where he lived, to Chirton Green. He died in January 1937 and
his wife Margaret died in 1940. The land and cottage were offered to the
Borough Council for the extension of the Ralph Gardner Memorial which was
erected in 1882. On the south side: I appeal to God and the world – Gardner.
On the east side: Who suffered countless ills, who battles for the true and just –
Tennyson. And on the west side: A faithful son of father Tyne – Dr Leitch.

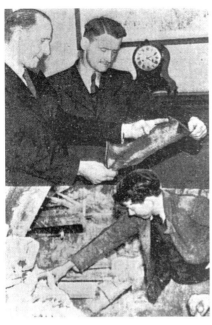

Left: The Borough Surveyors examine a Treasure Trove parchment dated 22nd May 1653 found under the stairs of Chirton Cottage in February 1948. *Below, left*: The demolition squad who found the parchment. There was speculation about this parchment because the house was rebuilt in 1856 and the document was found in such a position that it was bound to have become known if it had been there at the time of building. The parchment was written in red ink and told the story of an attack on the house by armed Magistrates Excise men. After the attack, it is said, had been beaten off with the aid of the captain and crew of the ship *Elizabeth*, it was decided to bury 900 guineas under a young sycamore tree in the grounds of the cottage. Workmen dug round the position indicated on a plan at the foot of the parchment and found no trace of the money. The authenticity of the document was doubtful as the first guinea was minted in the region of Charles II in 1663. Another point, the sort of wax used for the seal could have been bought in the shops in 1948.

St Joseph's RC Church on Wallsend Road in 1955. His Lordship the Right Reverend Joseph McCormack opened the church on 24th August 1955 with the Lord Bishop of Hexham and Newcastle. Joseph Austin Ord, a market gardener, owned the land and when he died he made a deed of gift of one acre of land to be set aside for a parish hall. Permission was granted for Father Kinleside to build a church hall in December 1934.

Hawkeys Lane Swimming Baths around the 1920s. The baths was used frequently, especially by the schools in the area. It was an open-air baths with cold water. It closed around the late 1960s or early 1970s.

The junction of Wallsend Road and The Quadrant in 1932 before the Ridges Estate was built. Gordon Brewis and Doreen Anderson enjoy the ride in these tin cars with no fear of traffic. Doreen diverted the boy next door, who owned the car, to ask his mum for a bread and jam sandwich. While he was indoors, she jumped in his car and took off.

S. Burn is the name above the shop, a fruiterers and florist, and occupied by N. Zonakas, on Front Street in 1938.

The Milburn Toffs parading on Front Street. The date is approximately 1936.

Edward Dodd outside his home in Wooler Avenue, West Chirton Estate in 1947. The first recorded entry for West Chirton Hall was in 1825, Michael Robson Esquire as owner. The hall, a plain building built with brick, held 111 acres of land, with a plantation surrounding it. John and Mary Hedley lived at West Chirton from the 1860s to the 1890s and John became Alderman in 1890. At the turn of the century, Jason G. McIlvenna lived at the hall. The last recorded date was 1925, but the farm was being worked by Thomas William Lawson until about 1934. In February 1938, 6-8 acres of land was reserved for educational purposes. Norham High School was opened in 1973 on the site.

Construction of Stannington Road in October 1947.

A class of children from Queen Victoria School stand on Hawkeys Lane waiting for the Royal Procession to pass them on Friday, 29th October 1954. Thomas Hitchcock is 4th left. Patients in dressing gowns and blankets had front seats on the Queen's route outside Tynemouth Infirmary. The Queen wore a mushroom coloured fitted coat with a fur collar and the Duke of Edinburgh wore a single-breasted grey lounge suit.

The children from St Joseph's RC School stand on Wallsend Road waiting for the Queen to pass them on 29th October 1954. The Queen's tour began at Monkseaton Station at 10 am. The bells of Christ Church rang out as the Royal Procession passed through North Shields on its way to Wallsend Town Hall. They left for Sunderland at 5.30 that evening after touring round Tyneside.

Folk wait for the doors to open at Chirton Social Club on Silkeys Lane in the 1950s. Margaret Stewart and Dorothy Osbourne are two waiting. Chirton Club began with approximately 300 working men assembled together who agreed to set up a Men's Only Club and shares of one pound were offered. They bought an old wooden army hut and erected it on Silkeys Lane. There were market gardens and fields surrounded the wooden hut, not like today when the site is surrounded by Council houses. Members sat on wooden forms and drank at trestle tables; they had to bring their own pint pots as there were no glasses. The club's first secretary was a miner named Charles Scott. Mr W. Hunt was in the chair and W. Morton, C. Hunter and W. Towart were elected to the committee. Around the wooden hut, a fence was erected at the tremendous sum of £10 and it was known as the Golden Gate.

Front Street Chirton around 1969. Mary Robinson, second from right and her husband Len approaching her. The garage in the background was opened in 1965 by Mrs Hewitt. Her husband John opened Chirton Service Station five years prior on the corner of Front Street and Silkeys Lane. Behind the garage are the flats of Simpson Street.

Molly Mack, unknown, Mary Miller, Pat Ellis and Phyllis Siddell taking a break outside Clay and Sons, (Charlie Clays) Clothing Manufacturers on Norham Road around 1956.

Glyn Morgan Jnr and Graham Griffiths doing a spot of gardening on Wooler Avenue in 1968. Glyn's parents are Peggy and Glyn Morgan. Peggy was from Church Way and Glyn was from Wales. They met while in the RAF.

Collingwood Arms on Front Street in Chirton in the early 1950s. A few names are known: The manager Stan Hewitt, Mrs Welsh, Peggy Welsh, Ann Matthews, Mrs Milsip, Mrs Walsh, Mrs Kitty Hunter, Dorothy Denley and Mr Dolton.

An advert for the Collingwood Arms.

Mine host has spent all his life in the Trade

Mr. Stanley Johnson, manager.

Our photograph shows the spacious bar to advantage. There is a special alcove for darts players.

MANAGEMENT of the Robin Hood is quite a family affair. Fifty-nine-year-old Mr Stanley Johnson is helped by his wife, Elizabeth.

Also assisting in a part-time capacity is 24-year-old Brian Sanderson, a grandson of Mr and Mrs. Johnson

Mr Johnson has been in the licensing trade all his life — and the whole of that time has been spent in North Shields.

After 30 years at the Dolphin, the Phoenix and the Colonel Linskill, he moved to the old Robin Hood nine years ago.

But this one is the first entirely new public house he has been given during the 39 years behind the bar.

And what does he think of his new quarters?

"They are nice—very, very nice. It is wonderful to be able to look after a lovely place like this," he says.

Attractive modern furnishings make the buffet just the place for a quiet drink and chat.

JOHN ROWELL & SON
LIMITED
HIGH STREET - - - GATESHEAD

have pleasure in announcing the opening of

THE
ROBIN HOOD INN
FRONT STREET - - - - CHIRTON

"The Robin Hood Inn," Front Street, Chirton, is situated in one of the most modern residential areas of the town and Messrs. John Rowell and Son Ltd., have kept this in mind in erecting their new hotel. They have endeavoured to provide the most modern amenities to attract a discerning clientele.

Comfort, elegance and good taste are apparent in each department where air conditioning and central heating are combined for the customers' benefit.

Prize Medal Ales and the finest Wines and Spirits for which this Tyneside Company are renowned, will surely attract the connoisseur.

A newspaper cutting and advert for the Robin Hood Inn on Front Street in February 1959. At this time the manager, 59 year old Stanley Johnson and his wife Elizabeth had been in the licensed trade for 39 years. They moved to the Robin Hood Inn in 1950.

PERCY MAIN AND
ITS PEOPLE

Coble Dene, *circa* 1870s, before the Albert Edward Dock was completed and opened on 21st August 1884 by the Prince of Wales, after whom the dock was named. Chirton Dene ran freely near Silkeys Lane and, on the west side of Chirton, the Red Burn began a few hundred yards north of Murton Row, also ran freely and both entered Coble Dene. Coble Dene was a wooded ravine close to the River Tyne teeming with buttercups and sea daisies and with a shallow bed of rounded pebbles. The speckled trout once slumbered beneath the stones. On the north side down to the river's edge, a pleasant sight of whitewashed cottages and fruitful gardens covered the hillside. On the west of Coble Dene, green fields and waving corn gave a touch of quiet beauty and provided a pleasant retreat. This was so until the year 1811 when Burdon Main Colliery was opened. The scenery was sadly ruined, utterly destroyed with accumulation of enormous mounds of debris which fouled the Dene as pit pumps continually poured out their dirt.

Aerial view of the River Tyne, Smiths Docks, west end of North Shields, Meadow Well, Percy Main and the Balkwell. West Chirton Trading Estate had not been built at this time, they began building in 1938. Howdon is at the far left corner.

Inside St John's Church around the 1900s. The Lord Bishop of Durham consecrated St John's on 2nd September 1864. The church was built of stone in the early English style, with a chancel, nave, aisles, two porches, a turret and two bells. The Reverend Arthur Tomline Coates BA held it when opened. Rev Coates lived at the vicarage on the Newcastle Turnpike Road (Wallsend Road)

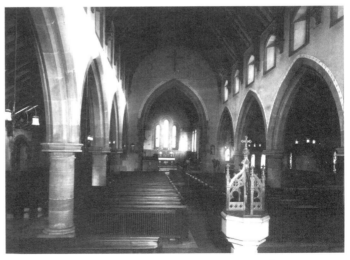

near West Chirton Estate for 32 years until he died in May 1897 aged 64 years. The Rev Peter McVities held the position for eight years, 1897-1905 and then Rev David Bryson (Daddy) for thirteen years, until 1918.

St John's Church. In 1920, Rev John Clucas held the position for 38 years, until October 1958, when he was 79 years old. He was a very popular gentleman around the community and was invited to many opening ceremonies including the ceremony at the Ridges Council School. The vicarage on Wallsend Road was closed down in 1955 and sold to Wm Younger and Co Ltd (Brewers) and Rev Clucas moved to the newly built vicarage next to the church. Rev John White held the position for 9 years, until 29th December 1968. The Rev Richard Barry Hicks BA held the position for 6 years, from March 1969 to March 1975. In September 1975, Rev Ian David Zas Ogilvie held the Parish until February 1978. The Rev Stephen Scott Huxley held the position for 9 years, until February 1987. Rev John Michael Pennington MA succeeded him for 7 years, until Rev Charles Henry Hope MA took over the position for the Parish of Percy Main in June 1994, keeping up the good work of his predecessors.

A certificate given to members of the Church of England Men's Society at St John's Church in from 1920.

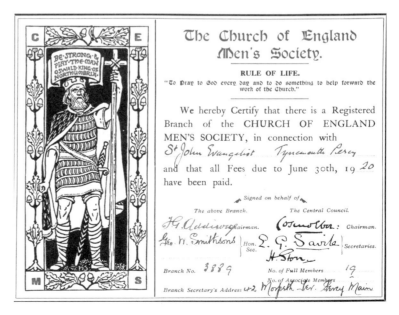

The Methodist Chapel and Burdon Street in 1973. The church opened on 22nd March 1902 and closed in the 1980s, due to demolition all ready started at Burdon Street.

The interior of the Methodist Church on Burdon Street around the 1960s. When the church closed, the organ was given to St John's Church.

A group of workers outside the Albert Edward Dock Sawmills during the First World War. (Or it may be the box factory, no one is sure.)

Fred Newton's butcher shop on Middle Row in 1938. The Newton family lived at 3 Burdon Street and had been in the business since 1873, over sixty years, starting with Stephen Reginald Newton. He must have died around the 1900s, because his wife run the butchers after that date until around 1929. From then, William Newton was ran the business.

An air-raid shelter at the
allotments on St James
Terrace during the Second
World War. Bob Bell and his
wife and friends stand in front
of the shelter. Bob was a
foreman fitter at the Tyne
Improvement Commission on
White Hill Point.

William and his sister George
Annie Fleming (aged 10) from
Percy Main in 1894. Annie was
christened George after her
father but was always known as
Annie. George Fleming started
up the business of Flemings
Painting and Decorating with
his relative Mitchell Fleming.
The business originated in a hut
next door to the Percy Arms
public house in the late 1800s.
The business was taken over
and is still running in Nile Street
under the same name of
Flemings.

Percy Main Station in 1965. Arthur Forrest and his sister in law Pat Appleton with her two children Martin and Carol Appleton.

Arthur Forrest and his wife Joan waiting on Percy Main Station in 1965.

A summer church fete in Percy St John's School field in 1960. A few names are known: Olive Jones, Sheila Thompson, Mrs Clements, Mrs Roper, Joan Balls, Jean Dodds, Emily Bradbrook, Jean McDonald, Mrs Bonemaker, Dorothy Nesbit and Mrs Dugdale. Percy St John's School was erected in 1975 but, in 1998, falling school rolls led the governors to opt for closure. The flats on Murray Close are visible behind the women; they started building 18 five-storey blocks at Hunters Close in 1957.

John Gardner, his wife and family outside their home at 1 Wood Cottage, *circa* 1890s. In the trade directories John was a general dealer in 1890.

Bill Fleming in the Auxiliary Special Fire Service in the old ambulance hut at the start of the Second World War. It was situated across the road from the Cricket Club, which is now the Homing Pigeon Club.

William English (left) standing with his work mate at Swales Wood Yard on Dock Road in 1956.

Billy White (who I believe was the stationmaster at Percy Main Station) with Martin and Carol Appleton in 1965. The Newcastle and North Shields line was opened in 1839 by London and North Eastern Railway. Electric trains began running in 1904.

George Fleming and his grandson Alexander Fleming outside his business on Station Road, next to the Percy Arms in 1920. In the Trade Directories (1890), George Fleming, painter, lived at 13 Brunton Street and then later he lived at St John's Street.

Celebrating the Queen's Silver Jubilee on Percy Crescent in 1977. Mr and Mrs Purvis, the oldest couple in Percy Main cutting the cake made especially for the day. The youngest resident, Morgan Quinn, is in his mother's arms.

SECTION THREE

MEADOW WELL AND ITS PEOPLE

Meadow Well Cottage, *circa* 1920s. The cottage was situated on the Meadow Well Farm for many years prior to this date. The first census in 1841 recorded that William Bell, a farmer, was living in the cottage. The Duke of Northumberland bought the farm for £5,800 by public auction in 1865. Completion of purchase was made in November 1871 and released on the 10th June 1875. On the 13th October 1932, Compulsory Purchase Orders were served to the tenants, Mr and Mrs Burrell, by Tynemouth Borough Council to make way for the erection of the new Ridges Estate.

The Meadow Well, *circa* 1900s, was known for its clarity of water. An old type of bucket pump was situated near the Meadow Well cottage on Waterville Road. In April 1935, Hull Museum constructed an old street and aquired the pump.

The Ridges Inn on Waterville Road opened its doors to the public in April 1940. It was designed to harmonise with the surrounding buildings and was built by Messrs Benjamin Peel Ltd from Tynemouth for the old established firm of William McEwan and Co Ltd of Fountain Brewery, Edinburgh, and City Road, Newcastle. The modern style of the inn

had rustic facing bricks and ornamental stone details. The roof of sand faced pan tiles gave a pleasing effect. The accommodation comprised of three large public drinking rooms, bar, sitting room and buffet. In addition, there was a shop for out-sale. An adequate and up-to-date lavatory accommodation was provided and a very large cellar under the building for the storage of beer. The manager, Mr George C. Murray and his wife Elsie, from the Lambton Castle in North Shields, occupied the first floor.

Hazelwood Avenue in 1934. At the far end of the avenue, among the trees, the old vicarage chimney pots on Wallsend Road are just visible on the horizon.

The foundations of Dahlia Gardens in the late 1930s. The crossroads is on Waterville Road and on the left is the Ridges Reservoir with, the house in front, the keeper's home.

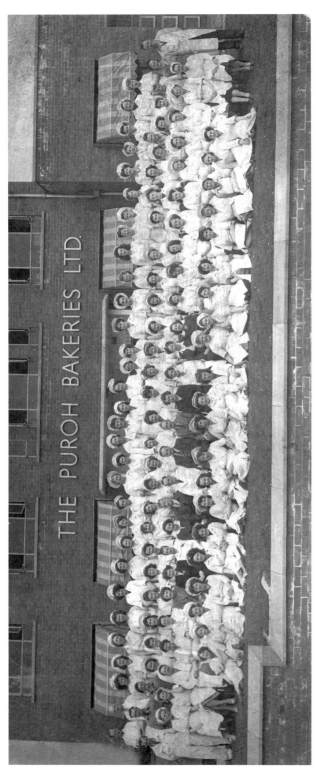

Staff of the Puroh Bakeries Ltd on Waterville Road around 1953. A few names are known, including: Elizabeth Moat, Doris Johnson, Esther Denley, Margaret Sexton, Margaret Buglass, Maple Crow, Nancy Crow, Belle Rippeth, Norah Grey, Mr Ions, Jean Wall, Doreen Tait, Maureen Rigby, Audrey Dennison, Mrs Williams, Isabella Boylen, Mary Little, Irene Henderson, Margaret Germaine, Audrey Lewis (née Foreman), Audrey Manson, Mary Patterson, Audrey Wilkinson, Elsie Burns and Alice Johnson.

Above: Isabella Lyall standing on Rosetree Crescent in the 1950s.

Left: Richard Rippeth on West Percy Road in 1951 at the age of 12 years old. Look at the appearance of the flats; wooden fences and metal-framed windows.

Above: Iris Hitchcock leans against a C reg Morris Minor on Maple Crescent in the early 1970s.

Right: Mr William Haddock and his granddaughter on Cedarwood Avenue around 1935.

Isabella Lyall in a tea hut serving refreshments on Tynemouth beach. She lived at Rosetree Crescent.

On Smiths Park field in 1975 is Lynn and her brother Mark Brown.

Two lifeguards, displaying their physique, on beach patrol at Tynemouth in 1960. Jack Anderson (left) and Jimmy Heads who lived at Cedarwood Avenue.

Petty Officer Norman Herron on shore in 1942. Norman served on the ship HMS *Woolwich* during the Second World War.

A Christmas card sent from the HMS *Woolwich* on the Mediterranean Sea at Christmas 1943. Wartime greetings cards such as this were a welcome reminder of loved ones overseas.

Greetings from H.M.S. "WOOLWICH"
Mediterranean XMAS 1943

Una Rippeth from West Percy Road joined the ATS in 1945 at the age of 19. Una is the oldest child of eight brothers and sisters. Her parents are Joseph and Grace Rippeth (née Foster). Una trained in Leicester and then was sent to Aldershot where she met Thomas. She was engaged to him in 1946.

Thomas Sproston at Aldershot in 1946, at the age of 20 years. Thomas lived at Cornwallis Street in Stoke on Trent. He was in the Army Catering Corp. He met Una Rippeth in the army at a barracks in Aldershot and they were married in 1948 at St John's Church in Percy Main.

Glyn Morgan (on left) was born in Wales and moved to Hazelwood Avenue after he was married. He was with the RAF in Cairo in 1940. While he was billeted there, he journeyed to Alexandria frequently to collect food from the Military Supplies.

Arthur Marsh joined the Durham Fusiliers in 1943 at the age of 17 years. He was billeted to Cairo in Egypt with his comrades not long after. Arthur is standing in the back bending over, he lived at Elmwood Road.

ATS at Maske-by-the-Sea in Yorkshire, Private Irene Banks is on the second row, second left in 1943. She lived on Marina Avenue.

Before we leave Meadow Well, here is an early glimpse of the area. This advertisement for Meadow Well Farm House Farm is from the *Newcastle Journal* of March 1848, from Thomas Hughes Esquire at Hylton Cottage near Coach Lane.

THE BALKWELL AND
ITS PEOPLE

St Peter's Church in Balkwell, on the corner of Central Avenue and The
Quadrant, in the 1940s. The Mayor of Tynemouth laid the foundation stone on
22nd November 1930.

The original interior of St Peter's Church in the 1930s. The windows are only partially filled in and it has no organ.

Sunniside was one of the streets newly built on the Balkwell Estate in 1921. Others included: Oswin Terrace, Burt Avenue, Eustace Avenue, Delaval Avenue, The Quadrant, Ogle Terrace and Balkwell Avenue.

Oswin Terrace in April 1941, a land mine dropped on the end of the street. Mrs Carr was the only one killed.

A bomb crater on Cartington Road on 10th April 1941. This was a familiar sight to those who endured the war.

Ethel and Matt Arkley with their sons, Stanley and Edwin, in their garden in Sunniside in 1940. Stanley was in the Royal Corp Signals.

Matt, Ethel, Stanley and Edwin Arkley outside their home in Sunniside about 1925.

Matt and Ethel Arkley outside their home in Sunniside in 1940. The sign attached to the wall stands for Stirrup Pump. It was a vital sign during the war for the fire brigade, so they could reach the pump in a very short time when they required water for fires.

Edwin Arkley joined the RAF in 1941 when he was eighteen. He was Aircraftsman Second Class. He remained in Blackpool for six weeks, square bashing on the beach and he then was billeted near Bognor Regis.

Sunniside in 1947, Edwin Arkley and his fiancé, Margaret Malcolm were members at the YMCA Cycling Club. They went on bike rides on bank holidays and picnics, to as far as Morpeth, Hexham and Durham. They were married in 1949.

St Peter's in the Balkwell showed the pantomime 'Dick Whittington', between the 15th-20th January 1951.

A marriage scene performed by the St Peter's Players on 1st March 1949. In the photograph are: Doreen Anderson, Jenny Taws, Alf Mills, Jean Chisholm, David Arnold, Jean Snord and Nancy White.

The Christmas Pantomime 'Cinderella' was shown at St Peter's Church Hall on Central Avenue in 1960.

BALKWELL COMMUNITY WELFARE ASSOCIATION YOUTH CLUB

PRESENT

IRENE STAPLEY
and
VALERIE MAITLAND

IN

"CINDERELLA"

A XMAS PANTOMIME IN 7 SCENES
BY LES BRIGGS.

FOR SIX NIGHTS
COMMENCING
MONDAY, JANUARY 11th 1960.
At 7-15 p.m. prompt

MUSIC BY :- Mrs. M. DONKIN.
DANCES ARRANGED BY :- Mrs E. CRAGGS.
REFRESHMENTS AVAILABLE AT MODERATE CHARGES

ADMISSSION ADULTS 2/- (2/6 Bookable)   CHILDREN 1/-

A confirmation group at St Peter's Church in the 1950s.

Celebrating a Coronation Revue at St Peter's in 1953. In the photograph are: Sheila Anderson, Margaret Richardson, Margaret Bolam, Jean Chisholm, Evelyn Brown and Betty Hart.

Construction of Balkwell Avenue in October 1946.

Construction of Wark Avenue in October 1947. At this time the Borough Council started building West Chirton Estate.

Aerial view of Chirton and Balkwell around the late 1930s. Chirton was once known as a rustic village and yet, well known celebrities lived there, including: Ralph Gardner, the Collingwood family, Duke of Argyle, Archibald Campbell and also names such as, the Reeds, Milbournes, Lawson, Alderman John Spence and Alderman Robert Hogg who were influential figures of their time. Balkwell was built by the local authority as part of their plans to do away with the run-down original settlement at North Shields. A plan to move the inhabitants to the Balkwell Farm was interrupted by the First World War. In 1919 they began building again.

We end this visit to the Balkwell with a lovely picture of Stanley and Edwin Arkley in their home in Sunniside about 1924. They were listening to the early (cat's whisker) wireless.

SCHOOLDAYS

Percy St John's School at Percy Main in the 1920s with Mr Myers the teacher. Included are: Andrew Foster, May High, Olga Pickering, Ralph Foster, Charlotte Foster, Ethel Dunn, Mary High, Tissy Dunn and Cliff Irvin.

Percy St John's School in the 1920s with Miss Clark the teacher. Included are: John Foster, Olga Pickering, Peggy Stapley, Nancy Clark, Dolcie Short, Vera Gunn, Joe Skipsey and Norman Nurser.

A Christmas party at Collingwood School on 19th December 1929. Jeffrey Park and Tommy Rutherford are two names that are known.

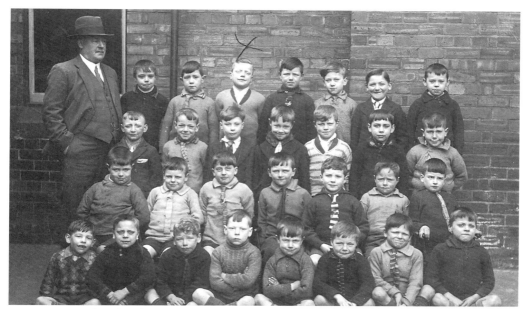

Eastern Board School on Albion Road around 1933-34. Back row, 3rd left, is William Walker.

Chirton Junior School at Billy Mill Lane on Empire Day, May 1939. Mr Bernard was the master for the school in 1934. The Rex Cinema stands behind them. It served many folk around for enjoyment on an evening out. Chirton School was hit by the Luftwaffe during the Second World War, suffered extensive damage and was demolished.

Empire Day for Chirton Junior School in May 1939. Chirton School is recorded in Trade Directories in the 1870s, with Margaret J. Smith and accommodation for 329 children.

Western Board School at Burden Main Row in the late 1940s. A class of boys in the school yard. Back row: Rubin Hall (1st right) and Thomas Wright (2nd right). Middle row: Ronnie Stonebanks (1st right) and Paddy McKeown (2nd right). Also included are: Roy Curry, Brian Colesby, Brian Dunn and Joseph Blacklock.

Empire Day, 1954 at Queen Victoria School on Coach Lane. Included are: Rose Mary Dixon, Mary Wrigley and Maureen Bradley.

A class of girls at Western Board School about 1950-51. Back row, from right: Margaret Crossland, Dorothy ?, Lilian Hardy, Ellen Wright, Betsy Wilson, Dorothy Tait, Dolcie Downey and Maureen Waterson. Middle row: Margy Vasse, Maureen Elgie, Rita Henderson, Margaret Rowley, Margaret Hewitson, Thelma Weeks and Carol Coin. Front row: Eileen Lough, Margaret Wilson, Sylvia Stoneman, Jean Haggerston, Joyce Chambers, Maureen Maniham and Doreen Wells.

Ralph Gardner Secondary Modern School in the 1950s. Mr D. Lawrence is the class teacher. The boys include: Eddie Pringle, Tom Wright and Brian White.

Kettlewell Infant School on Upper Toll Street in 1931. Una Jane Rippeth is on 3rd row, 2nd right, wearing a white dress.

A class of children dressed in Welsh clothing parade outside St Joseph's RC
School on Wallsend Road on Empire Day in 1954.

A group of girls dressed in Irish clothing outside St Joseph's School on Empire
Day in 1954.

Western Board School in 1958. Only a few children's names are known: Eric Heath, Elizabeth Cosh, Elizabeth Ferguson, Violet Burns, Elizabeth Errington, Keith Main, Irene Wilson, Irene Turnbull and Joan English.

Collingwood Junior School on Balkwell Green in 1961. Included are: Joseph Lacy, Brian Boyer, Dennis Barrington, Philip Dick, Susan Cull, Lorraine Heaps, Moira Belshaw, Joan Clark, Joan Wears, Maureen Smith, Vivien Brown, Lynne Skipsey, Janice Richardson, Pat Weatherstone, Ellen Peters, John Watson, Gordon O'Keef, Stanley Stevenson and Freddie Fox.

Queen Victoria School in 1963-64. Front row: 1st left, Diane Dekker and 1st right, Margaret Bishop.

Queen Victoria School in 1962. Included are: Christina Snowdon, Yvonne Sturmey, Christine Evans, Moira Ward, Jacqueline Bell, Lynn Barren and Ellen Wilson.

Spring Gardens School at Spring Terrace in 1964. Included are: Ann Walker, Nora Dowse, Mr Blackshaw the teacher, Vivien Payne, Moira Ward, Paul Wilson, Ian Harvey, Christine Evans, Yvonne Sturmey and Steven Swan.

Spring Gardens School about 1963. Only a few children's names are known: Brenda Wilson, Yvonne Sturmey, Vivien Payne, Paul Wilson, David Canon and Sidney Brown.

Linskill Secondary Modern School in 1965-66. Included are: Isabel McGinty, Yvonne Davidson, Catherine English, Susan Bush, Vivien Robson, Linda Scurr, Moira Ward, Yvonne Sturmey, Vivien Shaw, Brenda Churnside, Ann Lowry, Dawn Hughes, Susan Chater and Judith Nee.

Ralph Gardner Secondary Modern School in 1967. Back row: Glyn Morgan, Neil Armstrong, unknown, unknown, unknown, Peter Cash, unknown, unknown, Les Darrader, unknown and Sam Sorkel. Middle row: unknown, Micky Ingleby, Bob Grey, Norman Crosby, Brian Dickson, unknown, Harry Hearons, Archie Brunton, Des Baldwin and Ken Turner. Front row: unknown, George Armstrong, John Ishamor, Ronnie Brown, Mr Butler, Alan Brookes, Stefhen Matuszewski, unknown and David Hartfield.

Linskill Secondary Modern School in 1968. Front row: Yvonne Sturmey, Dawn Hughes, unknown and Ann Lowry. Middle row: Yvonne Davidson, Isabel McGinty, Judith Nee, Linda Scurr, unknown, Vivien Payne. Back row: unknown, Vivien Shaw, Brenda Churnside, Vivien Robson and Catherine English.

Fourth year girls at Ralph Gardner School in 1968. Included are: Hazel Rowley, Margaret Caush, Carol Armstrong, Ellen Peters, Lynn Skipsey, Denise Bradbrook, Dorothy Logan, Pat Campbell, Sylvia Browell, Linda Reed, Lynda Blythe, Olive Crosby, Joan Skelton, Stephanie Hearons and Maureen Smith. The teacher was Miss Shimman,

Ralph Gardner School in 1969. Back row: unknown, David Hartfield, Des Baldwin, Alan Brookes, Harry Hearons, Norman Crosbie, Brian Dickson, Ken Donnelly, Billy Boil, Ronnie Brown and Glyn Morgan. Front row: Billy Henderson, Stuart Harrison, Brian Miller, unknown, David Ornsby, Mr Crutchley, Bob Grey, George Armstrong, Stefhen Matuszewski, Sam Sorkel and unknown.

Ralph Gardner School in the early 1970s football team. A few names are known: Keith Heads, Jeff Watson, Comrad Lant and Ricky Harmen.

A concert at Queen Victoria School in 1971. Included are: Mona Ahommat, Richard Brown, Jamel Ali, Jackie Bamburgh and Brian Thewlis.

Ralph Gardner School in 1971. Back row: Brian Fairlamb, Rob Darby, John Errington, Rob Stewart, Alan Williams, Jeff Jewels, Ali Ahommat, Dave Falker and Paul Sales. Middle row includes: Maureen Bishop, Brian Hall, Billy Stanners, Micky Purvis and Gordon Griffiths. Front row includes: Mavis Smith and Grace Stewart.

Ralph Gardner High School in 1973. Included are: Gary Hussan, Comrad Lant, Julie Falls and Keith Heads.

Southlands School in 1968-69. Front row, 1st right is Elaine Marsh. Also included are: Susan Bell, Carol Howdon, John Scott, Stephen Reynolds, Kevin Elgy, David Noble, Willy Edwards and David Blakey.

Percy Main Council School football team in 1926. They had many successes due to the coaching of the team by the first headmaster Mr John Wm Cockburn, who was there for 37 years. In 1898 the school teams won three trophies that year. The school opened on 1st February 1892.

Robert Michael at Collingwood Primary School in 1968-69. Robert's parents are Diane and Bob Michael who lived on the Balkwell.

DAYS TO REMEMBER

A Christmas party held around the 1920s at the Albion Assembly Rooms on Saville Street. The picture is addressed to Mr James Walton from the North Shields Standard Permanent Building Society and was taken no later than 14th May 1928, as from the notes printed in the *Shields Daily News* he had went missing from his home at the Waverley Hotel, Whitley Bay. A hat, coat and letter addressed to him were found at the village of Escrick, near York. In the same newspaper dated 17th May 1928, his body was recovered from the River Ouse. The Assembly Rooms were part of the Albion Hotel, founded in 1853 and held many happy memories for folk in the area, especially for their dances, skating rink and a cinema. It burned down in 1985.

Joseph Auchterlonie and Alice Rippeth from West Percy Road were married at North Shields Registry Office in September 1957. The bride's parents are Grace and Joseph Rippeth.

The marriage of Billy Appleton and Patricia Nicholson at St Joseph's RC Church on Wallsend Road in June 1958. The children are: Hazel, Sheila and Cilia Appleton, Betty, Andrew and Mary Walker, Denis Appleton, Margaret and Ann Marshall. The adults, from left: Lizzie, Doreen and Audrey Appleton, Frank Fisher, Ronnie Appleton, groom and bride, John Andrews, Alice Slipper, Joan Andrews, Mary Walker, Philip Slipper, Peggy Andrews, John Andrews and Kathleen Marshall.

The marriage of Rose Dixon and Robert Crosby at the North Shields Registry Office in Northumberland Square in September 1969. The bride's parents, Stan and Lily Dixon, are standing on each side. Rose's parents lived on Marina Avenue and Robert's on Briarwood Avenue.

The marriage of Christine Morgan and Tony Porter at St John's Church in Percy Main, in December 1973. Christine lived in Wooler Avenue.

The marriage of Doris Torknor and Norman Brown at St John's Church in Percy Main, in summer 1975.

The marriage of Joseph Rippeth and Joyce Guttridge in 1957. The bridesmaids are Ann and Elizabeth Rippeth. The bride's parents are Mr and Mrs Guttridge and the couple on the left are Joseph and Grace Rippeth (née Foster).

The marriage of Thomas Arthur Sproston and Una Jane Rippeth (both aged 22) on the 2nd October 1948 at St John's Church in Percy Main. From left to right: Dora Westall Rippeth (Nana), Joseph and his wife Grace Rippeth, Burt Sproston (brother), the groom and bride, Joseph Rippeth Jnr, Belle Rippeth, Burt Sproston(father) and his wife and stepmother Annie Sproston.

The marriage of Cuthbert Hackworth and Karen Hopkins, at Tynemouth District Registry Office in Northumberland Square in June 1971. On the left are the groom's parents, Cuthbert and Mary Elizabeth Hackworth from Howdon. On the right are the bride's mother Belle and stepfather Robert Hopkins, who are from Limewood Road.

The marriage of Olaf Aspen and his wife Lorna, at Trinity Church on Trinity Street in September 1945. On the left are Minnie Barlow and Billy Harrison.

Around the 1900s, a group of men and women were on a summer day trip. Middle row, 2nd from right, is Margaret Turnbull (née Rutherford) from No 6 Appleby Street.

In the late 1930s Ossie Irving and Dorothy Tough being presented with a prize for tennis by Dryden Anderson. Also in the photograph are: Rev Forbes Horan (who later became Bishop of Tewkesbury), Bob Chisholm and Sheila Anderson.

Evacuees from the North Shields area, who stayed at Rothbury in the 1940s. The boy is Douglas Bell.

Margaret Brown, her husband Richard and son Clifford in the back garden of their home on Marina Avenue around 1946. Behind them appears to be an Anderson Air Raid shelter.

Yvonne Sturmey hiding inside the changing tent with Stan Baker outside at Tynemouth beach in the 1960s.

A family group out at Tynemouth Beach in 1959. Standing is Richard Brown, below is his son Clifford Brown and his girlfriend Betty Nicholson. Behind them is David Brown. They are all from West Percy Road.

The younger members of the Gallon family at Haggie's Christmas Party at Willington Quay in 1956. Front: Isabel, Doris and Catherine. Back: Joan and Ann.

Holy Communion for the boys at St Joseph's RC Church in the 1950s.

Holy Communion for the girls at St Joseph's RC Church in the 1950s.

The Coronation Day Revue at St Peter's Church Hall in 1953.

Members of the cast for the Coronation Day Revue at St Peter's Church Hall in 1953. From Left: Sheila Anderson, Margaret Bolam, Evelyn Brown and Jean Chisholm. The man in the middle is not known.

The pantomime 'Aladdin' at St Peter's Church Hall in 1952. Pantomimes became an annual event, performed by and for the people of the Balkwell.

A group of men dressed up for the boys' choir for the pantomime 'Aladdin' at St Peter's Church in 1952.

Glyn Morgan from Weyhill, stands in middle with his cousin, Robert Davis, (on left) and friend in Rassan, South Wales in 1963.

On holiday at Talking Tern in Brampton in 1962 – Johnny, Jacqueline and John Roper from Lawson Street.

A day trip to Flamingo Land in 1968. Alice and her son James Auchterlonie who lived in Howdon at the time. Alice before she was married was from West Percy Road.

A Flamingo Land day trip in 1968. Enjoying the elephant ride was Anthony (Tony) Brown and James Auchterlonie standing near. Tony died with Leukaemia the following year, at the age of four.

A visit to Flamingo Park in 1969 – Geordie Spears, Suzanne Maria Peacock, Jean Peacock, Stephen Spiers and Pamela Peacock.

On Tynemouth Beach in the late 1960s are: Annette, Thomas and Jeanette Peacock from Redburn View.

Easter Parade on Good Friday in the late 1960s. Joining in on Albion Road are: Keith and Jimmy Heads with their brother David behind them. They were with the Ridges Methodist Mission on Linden Road. The pub they are passing is the Queen's Head.

A birthday party for a nine-year-old Richard Brown and six-year-old Julie Brown on Briarwood Avenue in 1971. Included are: Richard Brown (sitting in middle), Margaret Brown (sitting on left), Julie Brown and Wendy Arrataki (standing right).

One of first and many Jazz Bands set up on the Meadow Well – the Cherrytree Raindrops in 1970.

Meadow Well Oranges and Lemons parade on Barmouth Way in the early 1970s. Sharon Shannon and Debbie McGill are 2nd and 3rd from the right respectfully.

Lynn and Chirton Jazz Band parading in Whitehouse School yard in the early 1970s. Mrs Doreen Edwards was the school's headmistress.

Charles Clay Christmas Party at the Bath Hotel in 1957. Only a few names are known: Mr Gosling, Mrs Barns, Mrs Marion, Geordie Chevington, Ellen Wright, Mrs Watson, Irene Watson, Mrs Chicken, Mr Grayling and Margaret Glasspool.

Charles Clay Works dance at the Bath Assembly Rooms in Tynemouth in 1958. Included are: Ozzie Armin, Brian Armin, Pat Ellis, Johnny Joseph, Omar Said, Mary Bell, Ozzy Mariana and Ellen Wright.

A group of men on a day outing to Jesmond Dene around 1924. First on the left is John Gardner, a trimmer by trade.

A day trip to Edinburgh for the Michael family in 1969. The children's Auntie Ann, mother Diane, Dawn, Janice, Robert and Donna Michael.

Arthur Henry Marsh is the baby in his mother Annie's arms at a Carnival in Milbourn Place in the mid 1920s. His sister, also called Annie, stands front right.

British Railway Party held at the Percy Arms (The Railwaymen) on Station Road in 1967.

Percy Main Amateur Football Club in the late 1920s. Middle row, fourth from left, is Bill Fleming.

St Edwards Amateur Boxing Club in the late 1960s. Terry Patterson, a boxer, third from right in front, and Albert Robinson, junior boxer, second from right. Including are: Joe Cortney, Davy Robinson, Jimmy McGuire, Ted Rodgerson, Alex Dale, Bob Lowden, Robert Malloy, Alex Luke, John Rogers, Eddie Saint, James Heads Senior and Alan Heads.

PUBS AND CLUBS

An advertisement for the opening of the Redburn Inn on Waterville Road, 1956. The building was originally the old vicarage for St John's Church. The managers, Mr and Mrs Harry Moore, had previously been at the Woolsington Hotel in North Shields.

A group of men enjoying a sandwich and a bottle of beer on their yearly summer outing from Chirton Social Club just before the Second World War. George Heart who lived in Burt Avenue is on the right.

The Coberg on Tynemouth Road in 1949 – Geordie Smith, Harold Roper and his brother Johnny.

G. Hamilton, Tom Wright, Joe Courtney and John Whitfield enjoying a pint of beer in the late 1950s. The name of the woman in unknown.

Ethel Taylor Brown enjoying a bottle of stout in Chirton Social Club in the 1950s. She lived in Silkeys Lane with her daughter Mary, her husband Thomas Nathan and their family. Ethel had been a widow since 1917, when her husband Robert died in a pit fall at East Holywell Colliery.

The Lodge on Tynemouth Road in the late 1950s – Geordie Harvey, Jimmy Heads and Terry Legg.

A group of men enjoying a pint of beer around 1958. Included are: Tony Rodgerson, Joseph Rodgerson and Eddie Binks from Weyhill.

Uncle Tom's Cabin on Bedford Street in the early 1960s, with Jimmy Heads and his wife Ellen sitting in the middle of the group. Also included are: Todsa Brown, Johnny Keddy, Loll Greener, Cornelius Saint, Davy O'Neil and Gordon Crow.

The Clock Vaults on Bedford Street in 1960. Left, sitting down, is Albert Porter. From right: unknown, John Van-Ryan, Mrs Van-Ryan, Maureen Van-Ryan and Irene Porter.

A bachelor party at Tynemouth Club on Front Street in 1960. Included are: John Whitfield, Bill Hunter, Tom Wright, Alan Heads, Jimmy Heads, Bill Coates, Albert Kinnere, John Rodgers and George Heads.

A staff party at Chirton Social Club in the early 1960s. In the middle is Billy Sharp with his wife Doreen, and friend Peggy Morgan.

A reunion at Chirton Social Club in the early 1960s. Ethel and John Walker travelled the world in their seven-year absence from the family. From left: her father Thomas Nathan and Aster the dog, John Walker, Marion Best, her mother Mary Nathan, Ethel Walker, Grace Nathan, Mary Dodds, Harry Nathan and Paul Nathan.

The Neville on Railway Terrace in 1965 – Gerald Junkin, Bob Marshall and Hayden Morgan from Wooler Avenue.

The Pan Shop Club on Howdon Road in 1968. Jean and her father James Lyall enjoying a drink. They both lived on Redburn View.

Chirton Social Club in 1969, with Christine Morgan and her mother Peggy, Winnie ? and Dorothy Heads.

The Cresta Club on Camden Street in 1971. A favourite meeting place to all those who enjoyed a dance and a drink in the town. Here are: Maureen Agnew, Linda Nathan and Yvonne Sturmey.

The Pineapple Inn mixed darts in the 1970s on Wallsend Road – Tot Office, Peter Wilkinson, Arthur Brannen, Micky Walker, Eddie Howell, Ralphie Redpath, Yvonne Robinson, Dahlia Smith (manageress) and Tommy Peacock.

James Pedigrew Gilgallon at the Roselyn Hall (Buffs Club) on Stephenson Street on 26th November 1976. He is wearing his medals of honour on his lapels. The sash he wears is the Knight Order of Merit and the Knight and Primo Medals.

Trevor Lyall, Terry Wright and Dave Patten in the Lambton Castle on Wellington Street West in 1971.

Jackie Hurne, Arthur Marsh and
friend from the Territorial Army
enjoying a bottle of Newcastle's
finest beer in the 1950s. Arthur was
from Elmwood Road.

In front of the dartboard enjoying a
pint are Arthur Henry Marsh and
George Stookie at the Alnwick
Castle in the 1960s.

Danny Brown and Arthur Marsh on the other side of the bar at the Alnwick Castle, Saville Street, in the 1960s.

Arthur and Davy Marsh in The Ballarat on Borough Road in the 1960s.

PEOPLE

Mary Brown (née Ewart) with her four sons,
James, Robert Ernest, Joseph and John
Alexander, *circa* 1880s. Mary's husband was
James Brown from Chirton.

Outside their home at 1 Wood Cottage in Percy Main are Thomas, Annie May, baby Olive May, John, Thomasina and Elizabeth Gardner, *circa* 1904.

Rosie Snowdon sitting outside her home in Chirton, *circa* 1910.

Right: Kitty and Edward Raffle
with grandson Billy, *circa* 1914.
The Raffles lived on Camden Lane.

Mary Sangster, her son Charles Junior, Bunty the dog and stepmother Kitty
Raffle. Mary lived on Church Way, in January 1932.

Elizabeth Herron, *circa* 1910. She married George Herron, and they had a daughter, Mary Elizabeth, who was born in December 1914. The family moved to Woodlea Crescent when the estate was built. Mary left school in 1928 and was employed as housemaid for Mrs Copeland in Tynemouth. Mary married George William Pearson in October 1937 at St John's Church in Percy Main. She died in July 1990, her husband George died in March 1996.

Mary Elizabeth and her mother Elizabeth (Lizzy) Herron who lived in Stephenson Street in 1917.

Mary Sangster and her two children, Margaret and Charles outside their home on Church Way in 1933. Church Way stretched from Albion Road to Union Street.

Bob Raffle, his wife Georgina and daughter Doris, who lived on Bedford Terrace in 1942. The photograph was taken at Saville Studios on Saville Street.

Olive May Wright with her two children, Tom and Ellen Greve , who lived in Cedarwood Avenue in 1940. Olive was born in Percy Main, her parents were John and Annie May Gardner.

Thomas Frederick Peacock and his mother Elizabeth (née Johnson) at Saville Studios in August 1947.

Mary Sangster, Mary Ann Poulton (Nana Poulton) from Rosetree Crescent, with two Australian friends on Howard Street, around 1947.

Hazel and her mother Elizabeth Appleton outside her home in Briarwood Avenue in 1950.

Joan Cheshire, Pat Slipper and Joan Crow standing on Briarwood Avenue in 1952.

Bus driver, Teddy Boyle, Ken Taylor, Ellen Wright and Mrs Stanners on Woodlea Crescent in 1956. Ellen left Ralph Gardner School in 1955 when she was fifteen and started work in Charles Clay Ltd on Norham Road.

Jean Breavers under her umbrella in Woodlea Crescent in the late 1950s.

Ann and Betty Rippeth outside their home on West Percy Road in 1950.

Thomas and Mary Ethel Nathan (née Brown) outside their home in Silkeys Lane in the 1950s.

Johnny with his brother George Roper at Dockwray Square in 1934. Dockwray Square was named after Reverend Thomas Dockwray, the son of Josias Dockwray and Elizabeth (née Toll). The square was built in 1787.

Inside her home on Peartree Crescent around the late 1950s, Cathy Ellis and her ten children. Back, from left: Brian, Kenny and Joseph. Front: Lynn, Carol, Susan, John, Stephen, Cathleen and Charles.

Billy, Carol, Christine and Norman Gunn at Briarwood Avenue in the early 1950s.

Johnny Roper and John Styverson who lived in Knott's Flats in October 1948. Knott's Flats were built in the late 1930s, named after Sir James Knott, a shipowner.

Stanley (18 months) and Rose Mary Dixon (3 years) on the Library Stairs, Harbour View, Howard Street in 1952. They lived at 63 Marina Avenue with their parents.

Karen Rippeth, Patricia and her sister Linda Nathan on their Uncle Joe's new scooter on West Percy Road in 1958. Standing across the road is Clifford Brown.

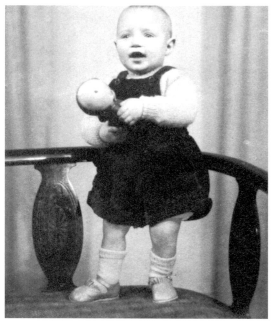

Lorraine and John Roper who lived on Penman Street in the 1950s.

Alexander Sangster from Howdon Road, *circa* 1920. He brought up his children on Albion Road where The Oddfellows now stands.

Bernard Johnson holding a dog, Jimmy Heads and his brothers David and Keith, on Oakwood Avenue around 1965.

Ellen Crowe Greve, with her children August Stefhen and Arthur John at Milburn Place around 1920-21.

Thomas Gardner (left) and his brother (sitting in the pram) in Sibthorpe Street around 1940. The names of the other boys are not known, are in the back yard and the outside netty (toilet) behind them.

Around the 1930s, Thomas Walker, from Milburn Place, with his pigeon ducts.

Bill Walker, Kevin and Carol Rodgers and James Heads outside Knotts Flats in the early 1960s.

Two-year-old Paul Bine standing on the wall outside his home in Briarwood Avenue in 1965.

Jacqueline and Pamela Peacock, unknown, Thomas Peacock and Stephen Keithlaw sitting on a wall in Cherrytree Gardens in the late 1960s.

Philip Weir, Pamela, Annette, Thomas and Jackie Peacock, and Elizabeth Weir on Cherrytree Gardens around 1967.

Lesley Nicholson, Paul Kerrigan, Graham and Norman Thorpe, and Christine Morgan standing in a back garden on Wooler Avenue in 1968.

Ian Toby and Gary Shannon, best buddies, standing on Barmouth Way in the early 1970s.

Jimmy Warrener inside his mother's home on Dorkin Avenue, enjoying the New Year. Later he was diagnosed with cancer and has died recently.

Sarah and Robert Dodds Westall with their son Robert Atkinson
Westall around the First World War. Sarah Westall (née Mason)
was born in 1877 and her husband Robert born in 1876. They
were married at the turn of the 20th century and had one boy
Robert in 1901, all their others were stillborn.

Una Jane Rippeth, age 6 years old, at Saville Studios in August 1932. She lived on Upper Toll Street. Una's family moved to Elmwood Road in 1934 as they were overcrowded. Her parents, Joseph and Grace Rippeth, had four children at this time.

Una's sister Belle aged three in 1930.

GLIMPSES OF OLD NORTH SHIELDS AND ITS PEOPLE

Annie May Gardner standing at the door of her shop at Charlotte Street, *circa* 1920. Her husband John was also a general dealer in Percy Main.

A stable yard in Bedford Street (where the heart Foundation Shop now stands) used for the London and North Eastern Railway in 1929. Back row: Wilfey Smith, Charles Sangster, Mr Cozer and Bernie Elliot. Middle row: Bertie Millet, unknown, unknown, Alex Sangster, Mr Bell from Marina Avenue, William Richardson Jnr and Josh Smith. Sitting down: William Richardson Snr, the two next to him are unknown.

Men who worked at the London and North Eastern Railway in Bedford Street in the late 1920s. Including are: William Richardson, Wilfred King, Mr King and Charles Sangster.

Charles Sangster worked for the LNER in Bedford Street, in the late 1920s.

Three stokers from the HMS *Granter* in 1949 – Mr Simmington, Johnny Roper from Knotts Flats and Tommy Dillon. Johnny's fellow workers, who were once pitmen, were from Whitley Bay.

Johnny Roper, a stoker, who worked on the *Colchester*, a coaster, in 1948.

Minnie, wife of Johnny Roper, and her son John outside the back entrance of Thompson's Red Stamp Store, where she worked, on Prudhoe Street in 1957.

Sergeant Robert Charles Sturmey in the Royal Artillery, based at Salisbury in 1954. The photograph was taken in Cypress where he was stationed for a time. After leaving the army he lived on Albion Road with his wife Daisy.

Charles Sangster (1st right on front row) when he was in the Royal Horse Artillery, during the First World War. Charles lived at Church Way.

Bob Raffle from Bedford Terrace, who was stationed in India during the First World War.

The foundation stone for the new hall of the Wesley Church was laid by the Reverend Harold Buxton on 18th July 1936. Another stone was laid for the extension of the building on 10th March 1956.

Wesley Church Sunday School on parade on Coach Lane on Good Friday morning in 1938. The outbuildings of Queen Victoria School are on the right. The church took a direct hit from a bomb during the Second World War and had to be demolished.

The harvest festival at the Wesley Church on Coach Lane about 1938.

This Poor Bairns advertisement was in the *Shields Hustler*, Easter 1923.

Carnival time on North Street around 1925 to 1932. The land around Middle Street, Front Street, North Street, East and West Street, and Milburn Place, had been owned by the Milbournes of Chirton House, but descended through marriage to Edward Collingwood, who developed the area in the  1780s. In 1936, the Council had begun demolition – through overcrowding of poorer tenants and health problems arose – and the community in this area was moved to the Ridges Estate. Most of the land was sold to Smith's Dock for storage.

Carnival time on Middle Street, *circa* 1925. Standing on the right side holding a crutch is Thomas Wright, nicknamed Crutchy, as he lost his leg when he was 14 years. The accident happened when his thumb was caught in a tramcar door. He was dragged from Dock Road to near Smiths Park on Howdon Road. His knee was badly scraped and gangrene set in.

Charles Foot's Preston Carriage Works, *circa* 1880-90. Charles Foot set up his business in Preston Village in 1851. In 1876, he opened these premises employing fifty workers.

A closer view of the employees of Chas Foot Preston Carriage Works, *circa* 1880-90. Back row, 3rd from left is Alexander Sangster from Albion Road.

Arthur Henry Marsh standing near his taxi outside North Shields Railway Station around 1970. He worked for Turnbull's Taxis and his car is parked on Railway Terrace.

Around 1936, Cathy Clements, Nancy Pickering, Lily Thompson and Jean Chisholm, standing in front of Billy Mill. Billy Mill once stood not far from the Coast Road, behind the old Canon Inn. Billing's Mill can be traced in the fourteenth century records of Tynemouth Priory, and a new stob mill was built in the 1590s. The mill was still in position in 1722, but burned down shortly afterwards. The stone tower was built in 1760. The mill came down in September 1967.

ALSO AVAILABLE FROM THE PEOPLE'S HISTORY

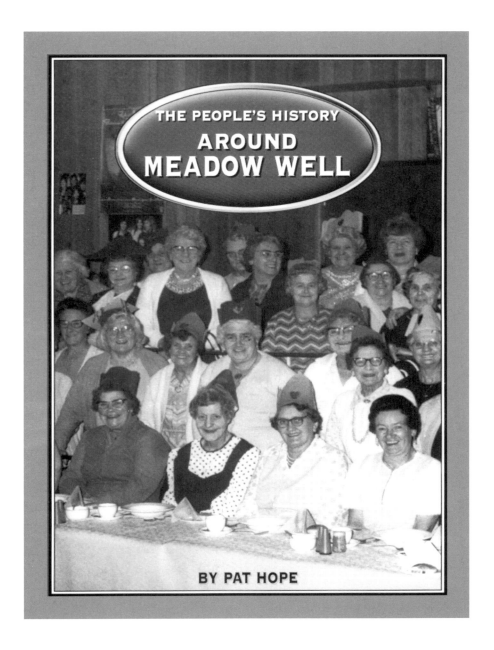

THE PEOPLE'S HISTORY
AROUND MEADOW WELL

BY PAT HOPE

Woman's Fellowship outing from Percy Main in 1960. Only two names are known: second from right, Olive Jones and seventh is Mrs White.

The People's History

To receive a catalogue of our latest titles send a large SAE to:

The People's History
Suite 1
Byron House
Seaham Grange Business Park
Seaham
County Durham
SR7 0PY